Elizabeth Taylor
A Loving Tribute

Cindy De La Hoz

PHOTOGRAPHS FROM THE
JOSEPH P. CRUZ COLLECTION

RUNNING PRESS
PHILADELPHIA · LONDON

to Jenny

© 2011 by Running Press
Published by Running Press,
A Member of the Perseus Books Group

All rights reserved under the Pan-American and International Copyright Conventions
Printed in China

Books published by Running Press are available at special discounts for bulk purchases in the United States by corporations, institutions, and other organizations. For more information, please contact the Special Markets Department at the Perseus Books Group, 2300 Chestnut Street, Suite 200, Philadelphia, PA 19103, or call (800) 810-4145, ext. 5000, or e-mail special.markets@perseusbooks.com.

ISBN 978-0-7624-4454-0
Library of Congress Control Number: 2011926254

E-book ISBN 978-0-7624-4458-8

9   8   7   6   5   4   3   2   1
Digit on the right indicates the number of this printing

Designed by Amanda Richmond
Typography: Tamarillo, Neutra, and Clarendon

Running Press Book Publishers
2300 Chestnut Street
Philadelphia, PA 19103-4371

Visit us on the web!
www.runningpress.com

Contents

Why We Love
Elizabeth Taylor ...

From *National Velvet* to *Cat on a Hot Tin Roof*, through eight marriages, White Diamonds, and years of tireless humanitarian work, Elizabeth Taylor achieved truly iconic status. She made her screen debut in 1942 and ever after the public has been enamored of the famously violet-eyed legend.

Elizabeth Taylor lived life to the fullest and never lost her sense of humor or her passion for living though she experienced numerous illnesses, a few bad movie credits, and eight marriages. Through it all her spirit never wavered and her star never waned. Why we love her is easy to see at a glance—we were astonished by her beauty, engrossed by her movie performances, and fascinated by her jetsetting lifestyle.

This tribute offers sweet reminders of why, for more than seventy years, we always loved Elizabeth Taylor.

...because we watched her grow up

Little Liz grew from child star to sexy screen siren

before the public's eyes in films of the '40s and '50s.

Born in Hampstead, England,

as a child

her smile brightened the English countryside.

ELIZABETH
TAYLOR
*A Loving
Tribute*

HER ANGELIC FACE

DEBUTED ONSCREEN IN

There's One Born Every Minute.

Braids were best for

National Velvet,

Elizabeth's first great movie.

SHE WAS READY FOR

her first kiss

IN THE MOVIE *CYNTHIA.*

...because she loved to play dress up

Elizabeth was a style icon of the first order.

No matter how many
accessories,
nothing overshadowed those eyes.

ELIZABETH
TAYLOR
*A Loving
Tribute*

Not her famous
PEREGRINA PEARL,
but dainty.

Belts accentuated her
hourglass figure.

NO ONE LOOKED BETTER

"dressed down"

IN GINGHAM.

Form-fitting
fashions
were a must.

Headscarfs,

knotted askew, enhanced her

star style.

...because she married (and divorced) Richard Burton twice

Since once is never enough when you still love the guy.

Of her
seven husbands,

it was the Richard Burton saga we loved best.

ELIZABETH
TAYLOR
A Loving
Tribute

. . . because she once had a pet chipmunk

Elizabeth's love of animals was renowned.

It extended to everything from . . .

a devotion to

horses

showcased in *National Velvet* to . . .

Chipmunks

THAT SHE BROUGHT TO MOVIE SETS, TO . . .

Pigeons

while on location in England.

SHE EVEN LOVED

squirrels,

AND THE WHOLE MENAGERIE.

. . . because she raised *billions* for AIDS research

Elizabeth's heart was as outstanding
as her talent and beauty.
Her humanitarian work was bountiful.

She helped start the
**American Foundation
for AIDS Research**
(amfAR) and created the
Elizabeth Taylor Aids Foundation.

Elizabeth used the power
of her fame for good, saying:

"Celebrity is not something
that comes without responsibility."

...because she had a
69-karat diamond named after her

ELIZABETH'S LIFELONG PASSION FOR PEARLS
AND PRECIOUS STONES WAS LEGENDARY.

Diamonds

may not have been her best friend,
but they were certainly good company.

Color-coordinated stones
**were often the perfect compliment
to her fashions.**

La Peregrina Pearl—

A $37,000 GIFT
FROM RICHARD BURTON IN 1969.

... because she could pull off a bob

ELIZABETH KEPT FANS GUESSING WITH
HER EVER-EVOLVING MANE.

She popularized the
short "Italian" look

IN AMERICA IN THE 1950s.

Hair adornments...

why not?

No one wore
"bed-head"
better.

ELIZABETH
TAYLOR
A Loving
Tribute

Parted on
the left side
was fabulous . . .

...*but right down the middle*
was equally epic.

A little snake charm?
Only for the Queen of the Nile.

... because she was friends with James Dean

... and Montgomery Clift, Frank Sinatra, Michael Jackson, and a dozen other men we love.

MONTGOMERY CLIFT AND ELIZABETH
WERE INSEPARABLE AFTER

A Place in the Sun.

Her famous friendship with Rock Hudson

led to her AIDS activism.

...because she made us afraid of Virginia Woolf

Sure she was a great beauty, but also had serious acting skills to back up her fame and proved it in movies such as *Cat on a Hot Tin Roof*, *Suddenly, Last Summer*, and *Who's Afraid of Virginia Woolf?*.

National Velvet
MADE HER A STAR . . .

...but *A Place in the Sun* made us fall in love.

WE MARCHED DOWN THE AISLE WITH HER IN

Father of the Bride.

She kept her seams straight in

Cat on a Hot Tin Roof.

Playing a high-end hooker in

Butterfield 8

earned her first Oscar nod.

WHO COULD FORGET THAT WHITE SWIMSUIT IN

Suddenly, Last Summer?

...because she demanded $1,000,000 for *Cleopatra*

Talent, beauty, a huge heart.
What's left?—Oh yes, brains.

ELIZABETH
TAYLOR
A Loving
Tribute

Only she could bottle
the fragrance of White Diamonds.

ELIZABETH
TAYLOR
*A Loving
Tribute*

...because she was the best argument for eye liner since Cleopatra

That face, that makeup, those violet eyes—
none could compete.

ELIZABETH'S

peachy pout

WAS ULTRA ALLURING.

SHE PROVED THERE IS NOTHING WRONG WITH
gilding the lily.

Elizabeth's *Cleopatra* makeup
inspired her look onscreen and off.

It was all about the eyes—
liner, mascara, brows.

...because the camera loved her

She may have married eight times, but one of the greatest
love affairs of Elizabeth's life was with the camera.

*Young Elizabeth was always
ready for her closeup.*

... because she was "just like us"

Off-guard moments show she was just like us—
well maybe a little prettier.

SLSA 63

BETWEEN TAKES

she basked in the sunshine ...

...but fanned herself
when it got too hot.

She could be windblown
but unfazed.

She loved her cake

...and ate it, too.

ELIZABETH
TAYLOR
A Loving
Tribute

... because we almost lost her so many times

Elizabeth was a true fighter
through numerous illnesses.

THROUGH EVERYTHING
SHE SUFFERED, INCLUDING BOUTS OF PNEUMONIA,
A TRACHEOTOMY, AND HEART DISEASE,
ELIZABETH CONSIDERED HERSELF
"the luckiest woman in the world."

...because she loved us

From signing autographs to keeping up with fans on Twitter,
Elizabeth always embraced the public with open arms.